# My Sanctuary: A Place I Call Home

Written by Doreen Ingram

Illustrations by Josh Green

Eloquent Books

Interior design: J. K. Eckert & Company, Inc.

Eloquent Books
An imprint of Strategic Book Group
P.O. Box 333
Durham CT 06422
www.StrategicBookGroup.com

ISBN: 978-1-60911-480-0

Printed in the United States of America

# Contents

Chapter 1. Where Have All the Years Gone . . . . . . . . . . . . . . . . . . . .1

Chapter 2. New Beginnings. . . . . . . . . . . . . . . . . . . . . . . . . . . . . . .10

Chapter 3. Cozy's Story . . . . . . . . . . . . . . . . . . . . . . . . . . . . . . . . .19

Chapter 4. A New Friend . . . . . . . . . . . . . . . . . . . . . . . . . . . . . . . .24

Chapter 5. The Rescue. . . . . . . . . . . . . . . . . . . . . . . . . . . . . . . . . .32

Chapter 6. Learning to Be a Chimp Again . . . . . . . . . . . . . . . . . .38

Acknowledgments . . . . . . . . . . . . . . . . . . . . . . . . . . . . . . . . . . . .44

About the Author. . . . . . . . . . . . . . . . . . . . . . . . . . . . . . . . . . . . .49

# Chapter 1

# Where Have All the Years Gone

"Wait! Stop running away. It'll be okay. You're safe now," I said to the newest member of our group. "Don't you understand? Don't you know where you are? Oh...I see. You don't know where you are, do you? When I arrived here, I, too, was scared and confused. That was a long time ago. If you will allow me some time, I can help you. I did say you were safe here. My name is Joao and this is your new home, my home. This is a place they call a sanctuary.

"I know that you're nervous. Perhaps if I tell you my story, it will help you. I am old now, over sixty years old, they say. I was born in a Jungle in Africa. I remember I was a bit of a mischievous baby. My mother would hold me lovingly and keep me close, but I often found something wonderful to seek out. There were

1

these creatures that could float through the air! I have heard my humans call them butterflies. Oh yes, but back to my story. One day, as I was playing close by my mother, watching this fantastic 'butterfly,' I heard my mother call to me. It was the 'alarm' call I have heard before, but this time with much energy. I could hear the terror in her call. I came quickly. I hugged my mother tightly as she ran up the large, strong tree. As she was climbing, a branch tore at my back, but I hung on even tighter. I felt the burning, stinging of the scratch. My mother climbed higher. I heard loud yelling from the other family members. Everything was moving so fast! I was terrified. What was that loud noise? My ears hurt! The sound was like the cracking of a large tree. *Crack, crack, crack,* then screaming and more screaming! I didn't make a sound, just clung tightly to Mother. I felt a jolt, then Mother let go of the large branch we were sitting on. Down, down we fell. We hit the forest floor with a thump! I fell on Mother. It felt like my breath had been pushed out of me!

"Then they came.

"These human beings, as I now know them, they stood tall and upright, coming fast toward Mother.

"'Mother! Mother! You must get up! Run!'

"Then I felt the harshness of a human rip me from my mother. As I was being taken away, I watched as the humans pulled my mother's lifeless body into a cloth object. She was gone. I didn't make a sound as the human slowed its  pace now. The cracking noise was gone, and so was my mother. I was about to

begin a new life, not of my choosing. What followed then was, well, the end of chimp life as I knew it.

"Enough about me for now. Didn't I hear my humans saying they were bringing us another friend? Didn't I hear them say that the 'new chimp' was in bad shape? They told me you couldn't climb trees like the others here. They said you were in a small cage for more than ten years of life. Now I see. You are weak. You are small for your age, aren't you?

"The human that brought you here, he was kind, wasn't he? Yes, they call him Eugene. He got you out of that horrible place you were in. You will meet others like Charles, Themba, and Siswe that help take care of our needs. Good and caring humans. You will like Phillip, too! You will see him often! Well, now that you have calmed down, what is the name you have been given?" I asked.

The chimp in the room with me answered shyly, "Cozy. That's my name."

"Seems the story is always the same, but you can trust these humans. You will see, Cozy. They are not like the rest that you have known," I told him.

"Yes," said Cozy. "I guess they *have* been giving me things to eat that taste good and that make my stomach feel good."

I noticed Cozy was beginning to settle down even more now.

He continued, "I had something called a mango yesterday. It was so yummy! Where I came from, my human didn't give me good food to eat. Sometimes, my stomach called out with pains, it was so empty. It hurt and I cried. No one seemed to care. I was so lonely! I don't understand all this. But it feels better. Every day I feel better."

"Okay, Cozy. So shall I finish my story?" I asked.

"I'd like to understand what is happening," he went on. "Maybe your story could help me. As I listen to you, I guess I wish I could remember my mother, too. I don't think I want to remember anything anymore. When I think about the past years I have lived, my stomach gets sick, and I feel sad. I also feel very angry! I was feeling nervous when the humans you talk about brought me in the room with you. I haven't seen my kind. Well, I can't remember ever seeing my kind. Even you scared me!"

"I know these things will get better soon, Cozy," I said. "I shall continue. After losing everything I ever knew, everyone I loved, I was put in a small cage, about the size of the boxes our fruit comes in. I was scared and couldn't stop crying. My heart

was aching from loneliness and all I had recently witnessed. No one came to me except to throw some food in the cage at times. I wanted my mother. But she was not going to come.

"What happened to my family is a thing humans call the bushmeat trade. Poachers, these are humans that hunt endangered wildlife illegally, kill and eat chimpanzees and other animals. Sometimes they also sell the animals to other humans. They just don't understand that we feel pain and loss.

"If the humans that destroy our homes and kill our families only knew the agony of separation and the despair we feel. Would they leave us alone? I don't know.

 There is a thing called money. That's why my mother was killed. *Money.* They could sell the chimp babies for this thing, and that is what happened to me. I was sold to a circus company.

The humans taught me to do tricks. They made money by having me pose for pictures with them. They liked me to wear human clothes. I cannot explain in words how uncomfortable that was for me. We are not humans and certainly don't fit their clothing!

We moved often to different places. I was never allowed to climb trees anymore. That was one of the hardest things. I longed to run and climb. My muscles would ache for this activity. But I wasn't allowed to.

"The circus was very loud and frightening to me. There were other animals there, too, like lions, tigers, and elephants. We all had our part to play in the entertainment. They gave me cigarettes and alcohol that made me dizzy and sick. I got a lot of laughs when they saw me smoking. After a while, my body got used to these things, and I needed them more

and more. I was ashamed and humiliated, but took what these humans gave to me. I didn't know that they were bad for me. I just did what they wanted me to do.

"Then the circus could no longer make enough money, so they had to find me another place to live. That's when I was brought to the zoo. I am told I was about three years old then. It was in a place called Mozambique. In this zoo, there lived many other kinds of animals, too. I have learned in my years that many zoos are

good and are different from the one I was taken to. They do not buy animals that were captured in the wild or bought illegally. They take good care of their animals.

"My zoo was not good to me. Not everything was bad, though. There was the one day the zookeepers brought in another young chimpanzee to live with me. At first there were a few sniffs and then she began to groom me. That is the chimp way of getting to know one another.

"The keepers gave us food and water. That was about all. Oh, they did like to see me smoke cigarettes. They seemed to like this behavior. I felt miserable all the time. But as time went by, my cage mate and I became best of friends. We told stories of our pasts. What we could remember, that is. The memory of my beloved mother grew fainter and fainter. But I never forgot about the humans that I saw in my forest and that had put me in the cages. At least I had a friend. I was not as lonesome as before. Still, there dwelt in me the horror of that day and the feeling of helplessness and hopelessness. *Hope.* Yes, now that is a good word. It means being able to see good things in the future. Hope was all I had at that time, hope that I would see some of my family again one day, hope that I could climb a tree like my mother showed me when I was but a little one. *Tree.* That is a good word, too. I have wonderful memories of trees and good-tasting leaves and our nests that we slept in. They were soft and cool. The air was clean and fresh.

"None of these things I had at this zoo. I heard the cracking sounds often, just like the ones when I was so young. They called it war. This war broke out in Mozambique and lasted more than thirty years. Yes, I was there when it started and still there when it was finished. Food became more and more scarce. We were hungry most of the time. Many animals at this zoo died of starvation. We would beg the humans that walked by for food. During that time, my friend fell ill. She lay beside me and took her last breath. I barely got to say goodbye. Then the humans took her away. I was alone. For so long, I walked from one end of the small cage to the other, back and forth. I longed for exercise. My joints hurt from laying on the hard surface for so many years. I felt myself get weaker and weaker. I was not a young chimp anymore. I was old beyond my years. I had seen too much. With little contact from any living thing, I just sat. I wondered how and when this would all end. Why me? What did I do to deserve this? I couldn't answer any of these questions. Finally, I quit asking. I ate and breathed and slept. That was my world."

# Chapter 2

# New Beginnings

"I remember it was warm this day. No clouds in the sky, no cracking sound of what they call gunfire. Quiet. Yes, quiet for once, I would even say peaceful.

"It was just a clear, warm day. I was sitting, looking outside my cage, when someone came to visit. He looked different than most of the other humans I had seen. He had a warm, caring look on his face. I could feel something different about him, something that made me stand up on two legs and look into the eyes of this human through the bars of my

cage. His eyes were soft and safe. That was it. Oh, and when he spoke, it was softer than others that I have known. I backed away. All the way to the back of my cage as I usually did when humans stopped near me. I had learned of their tricks of holding food close in hopes I would hold out my hand. Not me, I knew better! I don't like to get hit or pulled on, so I stayed back. I didn't trust any human now. Why should this one be different? Why should he care of my plight?

"He left. I knew it! They are all the same!

"I felt myself feeling sadder than I have felt in a very long time.

"After many more warm days and nights, this stranger with the soft eyes returned. My heart began to beat faster. This time he came with others. They were also soft-spoken. I overcame my fears and got up and came to the front of my small cage. I was staring at one of them, then ouch! I felt a sting. Down I went! When I awakened, I was at a different place. Where was I? What were they going to do to me now? I was not feeling well. I didn't have the energy to live this life anymore. *I am going to die now,* I thought.

Instead, I was visited by the stranger in this new cage. He looked different, though. He had a white cloth over his mouth. Much later I would understand that all new chimps had to go through an isolation period. The humans that took such good care of us had to wear masks and gowns. This was to keep sickness from being transferred to one another if there was any present. But back to the human. He still spoke to me in the soft tone, and oh, his eyes. Yes, it was him. I couldn't mistake those caring eyes. But what did he want? I had to admit, this cage I was staying in was bigger and clean, and well, wonderful!

They called it a room. I counted four walls in there. Two walls had steel bars that ran through them. I could see my keepers coming to visit me. There was a door in one of the walls. There were some climbing shelves that were perfect for making a bed of straw in. The temperature was very nice for me, not too hot and not too cold! I should also say that it wasn't

as wonderful as trees and grass, but good just the same. No bad smells, no loud strangers yelling at me, laughing at me, staring at me!

"This was different. Better, yes. I didn't know how long it would last. Would I go back to the small cage soon? I hadn't felt my heart beat so fast in a long time. Mmm! The fruit was scrumptious. The aroma filled the room. I was also given vegetables, fresh, good-tasting vegetables and bread. Bread is one of my favorite foods. My new keepers brought me so many good foods. I also had some ropes and could climb a little. It felt so good. *Good.* I haven't thought about that word for a while, but *good* was what I began feeling. The human with the soft eyes, Eugene, which I will refer to him as from now on,

came into my room for many days and many nights. He would sit and talk to me. I was scared. My eyes had seen so much by then. But as time went on, I began to see that things were very different here.

"I met another human. He is named Phillip. The one I had told you about," I said to my new friend, Cozy. "I

like him. He has a wonderful smile and hair on his face! I believe they call it a beard. I felt very safe with him. One day he came into my room. I don't know why, but I rushed over and embraced him with a hug. I felt so happy. I had to show him that I was so thankful to all of them. My family always hugged each other to show love and acceptance. It made me feel better when I was scared. So I hugged Phillip! To my surprise, he hugged me back! At that very moment, I knew my life was changed, but I had no idea just how different it was going to be!

"I was just getting used to this new room when suddenly I was being escorted into another area. As I was observing my surroundings, I heard a noise. I turned to see a small open door. I was afraid again. Just like you are, Cozy!

"There, stooping low in this small doorway was Eugene. He was holding out his hand to me. He wanted me to come with him. Unsure of my next move, I took a chance and decided to go. I took his hand and followed him through the door, trusting that I had made the right choice.

"I did! The sun was so bright, I squinted my eyes! It was the most wonderful thing I had seen, well, since I could remember. The smells, green grass! And look, trees!

"Holding the hand of Eugene, I followed as my feet felt the warmth and dampness of the grass. I smelled the grass and the dirt, and as I let go of Eugene's hand, I lay down. It felt good and soft. Again, Eugene called for me. I got up slowly for my

joints were sore and my body lacked energy. We continued walking until we reached some trees. Beautiful, beautiful trees! *Am I dreaming? Is this real?* I lifted my arm and then the other one and strained to pull myself up to a large lower branch of this magnificent tree. I sat there for a long time using all my senses to take in the smells, sounds, and feel of my new surroundings. Eugene had gone away for a while but came back and called me down. He walked me back into the building and into a room, different than the one I had been living in for sometime now. The same one that we are in now, Cozy.

"I don't know exactly how long I had been in the isolation part of the sanctuary, but I guess less than a season, which Eugene says is about three months. This new room was nice and comfortable. *Will I get to return to my tree?* I remember thinking to myself. I was anxious. I didn't sleep well. I had dreams that night. They were of trees,

my mother, other family members. I dreamed of a butterfly, just like the one I was watching before my traumatic change of life. I dreamed I was chasing this butterfly. I was running and running. I didn't look back. I just kept running, chasing this beautiful orange-and-blue butterfly. I stopped in the jungle. I didn't know where I was! I was crying, shouting for Mother! *Where is she, where am I?* Then I awoke. My face was wet with tears. It was a dream, just a dream. I was sad, but realized that I could still remember my mother's face. I could remember things from my infancy that I thought were gone forever. I went to sleep on my comfortable bed of straw.

"The next morning I heard the voice that I have come to love. 'Good morning!' he said. It was Eugene! I lifted my arm. *Please take my hand,* I hoped. I wanted to see my tree again. I wish humans could understand chimp talk. I

guess he knew just what I was thinking. The door opened, and out we went. I let go of his hand and found fruits and vegetables and nuts on the splendid green grass just waiting for me, and who is this?

Her name is Sally. Oh, you will meet her soon! She is very young and sweet. I was nervous. I hadn't seen another chimp in so very long. Right away, it brought back memories of my dear friend at the zoo. I closed my mind to this. I now had hope. I cannot go back and let fear ruin this time for me. Sally looked at me for a while and then came over and hugged me. My heart soared, and we both ate the delicious food that was laid on the grass before us. There were delicious red apples, mandarin oranges, bananas, and a fruit called pawpaw. I was happy! As I was eating my wonderful breakfast, I remembered my tree. I began to run, slowly of course, as age had gotten to my joints. I believe humans call it arthritis. Sally was ahead of me and had already climbed halfway up the tree. She was calling to me. I couldn't make it all the way up, so she came down and hung on the back of my neck. I almost laughed out loud with delight. That's kind of how it began. And that is how I ended up getting my nickname, Granddad of the chimps! Of course, being the oldest chimp at the sanctuary played a role, too.

"The place that we lived in was part of the sanctuary called the infant enclosure. I was going to be the chimp in charge of many more chimps to come here. I decided to stand up to the test and do my best to raise this new family."

# Chapter 3

# Cozy's Story

Cozy scratched his head. "I cannot tell you of my whole life story. As I have said before, I do not understand what happened to me. I remember this place, you call it a zoo. I believe I may have been born in one a long time ago.

"The next thing I do remember is living in a very small room for many of my life years. I was locked in a small box that had steel bars all around me. This cage, as you call it, was so small I could hardly stretch out. There was a man and lady who took care of me. After a time, the man did not come anymore. I was no longer let out of this cage. The lady locked it closed once and for all. She visited me at times, giving me food and water. Like I said before, I was hungry much of the time. I just sat or lay in my cage. Boredom was my only friend. My mind would play tricks on me. I would see shadows or hear noises that were scary to me. I would hear humans yelling outside the trailer the lady kept me in. I never heard any of my kind, just humans. I don't

**19**

remember much else except when the human with the soft eyes, as you talk about, Eugene, came and took me from that place. So you are right, I am not well. When I was there, where I used to live, I was very unhappy. Something inside me kept saying I must live, for what I didn't know. Is this what I was supposed to live for? I must tell you that I cannot control my emotions. Sometimes I get so angry. My past comes back, but I try to shut it out. Do you think Eugene will be my friend too?"

"Cozy, he saved you from the torment you were living in. Can you trust in me?"

"I'll try," said Cozy.

"Well, are you ready to go outside and begin your new life? Then you shall see what *hope* looks like!"

It was soon that Eugene brought Cozy out into the yard with us. As Eugene had done with me, he also did with Cozy. He took him by the hand and led him outdoors. At first Cozy didn't want to touch the ground with his feet. He was much more fearful than I had been. He was also so weak that he couldn't walk far. To climb a tree would have been impossible at this stage of his rehabilitation. Cozy made noises that were not exactly all chimp sounds. He also liked to stick out his tongue! I do believe I have even seen him suck his thumb. I am reluctant to say it was a bit comical.

Each day brought new challenges and greater strength to Cozy. He was beginning to put on more weight and muscle. He was getting stronger every day.

Even his hair on his body was thicker and shinier than before. Good health was returning to him.

Eugene spoke gently, hugged often, and eventually coaxed Cozy to climb to the lowest limb of a tree. Cozy was so scared but began to trust our human friend. Cheers would come from Phillip as he would watch the successes occurring. "Good job, Cozy," I would hear him say. This made Cozy work even harder.

Now there were three chimps, and the family was growing! Then three became four, and Zeena came to the sanctuary. In the future, she would be known as the Wild Child. You will see why soon!

When Zeena was an infant, she was purchased by a nice family. They did not understand that wild animals should be left to be wild and live the way God

intended them to live. They also may not have known that Zeena probably watched as her family was killed so they could purchase her for their pet. But they bought

her and were raising her like a human child. She wore little-girl clothes and had her own human bed and toys. She was confused and angry when she was brought to our home, here at the sanctuary. She kept to herself, not letting any of the other chimps play with her or even get near her. She was smart and

a very good and fast climber. Zeena learned quickly how to bully everyone around; everyone but me, that is. As I was resting in the sun she caught my eye. I saw her throw a stick at Sally. This was not the first time a stick went flying from Zeena's grip!

"Zeena," I groaned. "I will have to discipline you if you don't leave Sally alone."

"You can't get me, Granddad," she yelled back. Before Zeena knew what happened, I grabbed her and held her tightly to my chest.

"You must behave!" I released her as I felt that was punishment enough. She knew I was serious and stopped her bad behavior, for now anyway.

Morning came, and each time we heard those wonderful words: "Good morning!" It was Eugene, Phillip, and Jessica. Jessica was a beautiful human lady. I liked her a lot,

but Cozy did not feel the same as I did. I believe Jessica reminded him of the human lady that had locked him in the cage for so long. As we ran to the outdoors each morning, he would find a nice little rock or piece of fruit to throw at Jessica. I would discipline him when I could catch him. He had become quite fast these days. Jessica never spoke angrily to Cozy. She scolded gently and always talked to him kindly but firmly.

Much of the day I lounge in the warm sun in my tree. I watch the younger ones play. I think of what I missed as a young one. So much I missed. But I have so much work to do here. Taking care of my new family group and teaching them what I know will be a big job. Eugene, Phillip, Jessica and the keepers all help us to live the best chimp life possible at this place called Chimpanzee Eden. Life is good, and it is about to get busier!

# Chapter 4

# A New Friend

As we were all playing outside, enjoying the great outdoor life we had come to know, there was something going on at Chimp Eden. I could sense a change. As I have learned from experience, when Eugene leaves us for many days and nights, something new is going to happen here.

The story, as I have heard tell, is a chimp was in trouble in Luanda, Angola. Eugene and the team had gone to save him from a miserable life of abuse and neglect. They said that this chimp had been chained to a tree there for many years. He was named Zac. The place he lived was located outside a nightclub. That is a place humans go to dance and socialize with each other. Sometimes it is a bad and scary place. At this nightclub, people would give Zac bad things like alcohol and cigarettes, just like the humans did

to me a long time ago. They would laugh at him as he acted foolishly. He didn't know what he was doing most of the time. He was left outside in good weather and bad, left there when it was hot and when it was cold. We chimps don't like to get rained on, so I feel sure he was sick at times and miserable. He was malnourished and weak from being chained up for years. I would imagine this was very painful and uncomfortable for him. They say the neck collar he wore and the chains were very heavy.

Eugene got the permission of the government to bring Zac to Chimp Eden. After his three months in quarantine, he was introduced to all of us in the enclosure.I guess I haven't really explained the enclosure yet, have I?

Well, to begin with, we have our indoor night rooms that we sleep in. Our keepers make sure we have fresh hay to make our beds and sleep on each night, fresh food,

and water. We have everything a chimp could need! They even give us treats often. We love popcorn!

There are some doors that lead to an outside area. It is very large and has many

trees. It also has large areas of grasses and bushes. Plenty of room to run and play and climb, too! Sally's favorite place to climb is a eucalyptus tree. If you could see the tree's trunk, you would find that its bark is worn, since she uses it so much. She likes to be by herself most of the time for some reason.

There is fresh water in several areas of the enclosure. I love to get a cool drink from them during the hot days here. I chuckle to myself when I see Eugene placing these contraptions around. We are supposed to figure out how to get the water from them. We also have some wooden gadgets that the keepers stick fruits and vegetables on and hang in the trees. They call these enrichment devices. I always work them out very fast. That's why it makes me chuckle, because I am so clever, and they don't know it! It is a delightful place to live!

Well, back to Zac. Once we were properly introduced, I noticed that he didn't have much hair on his body. In fact, the poor thing was almost bald! I guess he had been so weak and in poor condition for so long that most of his hair had fallen out. I could see all his bones through his skin because he was so thin. His skin hung like something that was old. It was dry and cracked. I know that he was uncomfortable and in pain. He didn't communicate verbally much yet. Maybe he was still in a little bit of shock. He enjoyed lying in the

sun. Yes, he loved lying in the sun. Zac has a strange habit. He pulls a piece of hair out of his body, puts it into his

mouth, and offers it to you. I have learned with time this is Zac's way of saying hello. It is a way for him to see if you are a friend or not. I pull one of my hairs out and give to him. That pleases him, and it's his proof we are friends. I actually saw Eugene do the same one day. I thought that was amusing!

We, as chimps, groom each other a lot. What is grooming, you say? Well, it is a very important part of chimp life. We show our respect and love for each other in this way. We often look through each other's hair and pick out any insects, like ticks, for example. It helps in keeping us healthy. This also helps the family bonding process that keeps us close. I believe this comes naturally to us.

As time went on, Zac began to fit right in. It always takes a

while! As we were promised, five baby chimps were added to my family. That makes it a very busy day for me here. It does look like Zac may be in line to become the next leader of this group. I will teach him what he needs to be a great Alpha male like me.

Zac called out to me, "I'm glad to have so many friends now. These are the best days of my life!" I gave Zac a hug. Hugs are big around here. Cozy doesn't like them too much but will give one every once in a while when he knows he has been naughty. That is also a way we make up. Chimps don't stay mad at each other for long. We don't carry what humans call a grudge. We forgive each other and move on. We have to forgive Zeena a lot!

She loves to come and start trouble with us, as much trouble as she can get away with. She may have a slap at Sally or throw a stick at Cozy. I think she really wants the attention.

"Zac, did you know Zeena escaped once? She climbed up to the top of a tree, then over the tall fence she went! Oh…we were all so frightened for her.

"There was Eugene and Phillip to the rescue again. Eugene climbed a tree to get to her. Yes, he can climb very well! He gave a chimp call and down she climbed. When they reached the ground, she came right to him. I believe she was scared, too. She hugged him so tight. And guess what. That was the very

first hug she gave to anyone here. Eugene brought her back to us, back inside the enclosure. She came right to me and got another big hug from Granddad Joao!

"When the sun was going down, we went into our night rooms as usual. Zeena was still a bit upset from the day of drama she brought upon herself. She slept very close to Sally. Sally wasn't one to get too close to anyone except humans, but she allowed Zeena close that night."

Zac slept well after having a very busy day too. As Zac and Cozy and I made up our hay beds, we talked together. Each of us came here from a different place, but came here for the same reason. We needed to be saved. We needed help. We are the lucky ones. There are many more of us out there in confinement. So many chimps have been robbed of the life they were living. They were stolen from their families because of the bushmeat trade. As I have said before, it is a very bad thing. It is why most of us are here today. The humans that kill for money may not know any other life. It is wrong of them! Poachers are humans that go into our forests and kill animals that are supposed to be protected.

They can get into our forests easily because so many trees have been cut down and roads built. I know that the place we live, Chimp Eden, tries to teach humans about the bad thing, the bushmeat trade. All I can do is hope. Yes, there is that word again. *Hope.* This time, for me, it means that I wish that humans would leave chimps to live the way we were meant to live, wild and *free!* We live together in family groups in the wild. The members teach the young how to survive and grow strong. It is not an easy task. Without the family to pass on knowledge from one another, chimps in the wild may one day be extinct.

This is the life lesson I hope will be learned.

# Chapter 5

# The Rescue

"My story? Oh yes, I have one. Do I dare tell you? If I do, will they come back and get me? *Faith?* You say to have some faith, Joao? Hmmm...I look into your eyes, and I see knowledge and wisdom. I know you are a leader. You say I will trust more in time. I do hope that is true!

"I'll share our story with you in hopes another might benefit from it.

"Well, to begin with, I am called Sampa. I am six years old and my companion is Tony; he is only four. From our cage I could see many dwellings. Humans lived there and one of the families were our owners. We were starved. They

fed us two or three times a week. We had lived in this cage I speak of for about four years. To stay alive, I had to beg. I stuck my arms out through the bars of our tiny cage begging the human beings that walked by for something to eat. Many times instead of food, I got a slap or blow with a hard stick. It hurt, but I held my hands out anyway. It wasn't just me that needed to be fed. What about Tony? Yes, maybe it was Tony that kept me going. He gave me the strength and courage to stick my hands through the steel bars and beg for food.

We never got out of this cage. I often thought to myself, *Why are we here? What purpose do we serve?* Humans were afraid of us. Poor Tony. They shouldn't be afraid of him. He's just a small chimp. The human that sold him to my owners had clipped his canines and removed a few other teeth. He did it so Tony couldn't bite anyone. Tony said he had bit a man who was hurting him. He told me that this man had killed his family. I can't blame him for biting! He said the

**33**

man was hitting him. I know what that feels like. Humans have done very mean and cruel things to me too. I lived a happy life before the humans entered my world. The memories of that day are etched in my mind. At least I got to say goodbye. My Momma whispered to me before I was taken away, 'Have courage, my brave one.' She also was killed. I will never forget these words.

"I was Tony's protector now. He relied on me to get food for both of us. That is why I held out my hand, only to be beaten at times. I never gave up, though. I knew if it weren't for me, he would not survive. I needed him as much as he needed me. If he were gone, I might give up. I tried to have the courage my Momma commanded of me.

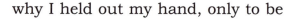

"As we lay on our small board, we would look out to the few trees that we could see from our cage. All we could do is hope one day to be released and run free once

again. We climbed on the bars of our cage for entertainment. Tony loved to hug and cuddle. No matter how bad things got, I could always rely on a smile from him. The smile kept me strong, strong enough to beg each day.

"Before our rescue, I'm told, a team of humans were trying to get some chimps out of Angola. They came across a man who informed them about me and Tony. They got to the place they had been directed to and found us. We were lying on two rotten boards. When we saw these new humans we climbed up on the bars. Right away I put my arm out. 'We've come to help you,' I recall hearing from the human you call Eugene. "Unfortunately, there was no key to the lock for our cage. Eugene returned and cut the lock off. I felt a sting and I went to sleep. I awoke to a new cage. Tony was already swinging on some ropes that were hanging from the roof. I looked around and noticed that we weren't just in a new cage; we had moved to a new place! The surroundings were quiet. This cage was at least ten times the size of our old one. It had a floor. Oh, it felt so good to put my feet down on solid ground. We were introduced to a human lady and given very good food regularly. My favorite drink was strawberry yogurt. We had a ball to play with and ropes to swing from. I thought this a wonderful change. I had no idea what was in the near future for us.

"After some time at this new home, Eugene visited again. He had a plan, but I was not aware of what it was at the time. He was moving us again but this time to

this sanctuary. Well, of course I didn't understand that at the time. I have to say I gave Eugene quite a fight getting into the crate we were to travel in. As a matter of fact, I am surprised he didn't just give up!

"It all started when he came for that visit. I admit, I trusted no one. But when he came into the cage and climbed onto the ropes like we do, I felt differently. I had never seen a human with chimp behavior! I liked it and I joined him on the ropes. He played with Tony and I for a few moments, then went outside the cage. He brought a crate to the entrance of the cage and called us to come in. Tony ran right in but I wasn't sure of this situation. He couldn't get me into the crate so he came in the cage with us. That didn't help either. I did not want to get into a small cage ever again and nothing was going to change my mind. Eugene gave me a drink and I began feeling a bit sleepy. But I was strong and could not be forced into the crate. He tried the water hose. He was squirting me with it in hopes I would get away from the water and run into the dry crate. Nope, I just kept hanging on to the bars of my cage. He gave me more drink. I got sleepier. Next thing I knew, I was waking up inside of the crate. Tony was with me, but I was angry. I did not want to be in that small crate!

"Eugene had only a few hours left to get to the airport so we could fly home to the sanctuary. He had no time to rest. He had to hurry to the plane. All we knew was that we were going very fast in the vehicle to get to the airport. We got to a place that was very loud. I covered my ears, which is hard to do because they are so

large. We were at the airport. We were then whisked away to a dark area in the airplane. I remember being shaken around a lot. We relaxed, happy to be together. I believe we fell asleep. When we arrived to our destination, I saw Eugene and some other humans that were new to me.

Their voices were calming. We were off again, riding in another vehicle. Well, here we are.

"Tony continued to stay right by my side. I am brave, and when we were let out to the enclosure for the first time, I went right out! Poor Tony, he didn't leave the cemented area near the door. Cozy decided he was excited about his new friends, so he ran over to Tony and grabbed a hold of Tony's arm. He slipped, and it pinched Tony. Tony cried out, and that was all I needed to run to him. I gave him a long and loving hug. He calmed down, and eventually we moved out to the grass. Tony held tightly onto my back. Finally, we got to see what we had just walked into. *Paradise!* That is a word I have learned from Joao. It means the best place you could ever imagine. We went running to the trees, following the others as they were racing each other to one of the fruit trees ahead. My dreams have come true. I am one happy chimpanzee!"

# Chapter 6

# Learning to Be a Chimp Again

We left the night rooms to go outside with the others. Eugene no longer needed to come into our enclosure anymore. I had become the true leader and help the keepers teach my family the things they need to be more independent. As always, there lying on the ground was all our favorite foods: bananas, pawpaw, eggplant, apples, and oranges. Everyday there is a different variety. My favorite food happens to be eggplant and macadamia nuts. Of course, I love bread. As the Alpha Male, I eat first. I grabbed enough to fill my arms and went to my tree log that I enjoy relaxing on. It was chilly this morning, and my joints ached. Sampa came over to me and asked for some of my food. I shared one of my oranges with her. She ran off to enjoy her sweet fruit. There was some commotion this morning. Looking over my shoulder, I saw Cozy running for the fence area. Every day, either Marc or Lize and sometimes Nenine bring guests by to say hello to us. Some stay for a short time and help the team to do chores around here. I believe they call them volunteers. Of course, they stay outside of the tall fence that separates us. As the guests walked by the fence today, Cozy decided to

throw some stones and one of his apples at them. One of the visitors jumped and squealed out loud. They were warned of this trick Cozy likes to pull! The tour guides and guests just moved on and continued the tour. I went over to Cozy and gave him a thump on the head!

"Hey, what was that for?" he asked.

"Cozy, don't you understand these humans help to make life better for us? You mustn't try to hurt them as they pass. You are only hurting yourself. Learn to forgive, Cozy!" I spoke sternly.

As we were working out the dispute, I noticed Jessica coming to the fence with some macadamia nuts. She sat on the ground, on the other side of the fence. It was learning time for the group. The team at Chimp Eden did this often to help teach us to be more independent of humans so that one day some of us might be released back into the wild. Teaching our group of the dangers of snakes, scorpions, and things of that nature takes patience and time. I sound the alarm call if I see any of these creatures so that I, too, have a part in helping my family learn. Foraging is a big part of natural chimp life too. Though we get most of our food from our humans, we eat the young leaves from some of the trees, and berries and fruit from a few fig trees in our enclosure.

"Look, Sampa," I heard Tony holler, "our friend is here!" Sampa and Tony moved over to the fence area and sat down. As Jessica threw some of the nuts through the

fence, it caught Cozy's eye. He came rushing over, hooting and hollering (that's chimp language). As he ran, he did a flip in the air and landed back on his feet.

"Better watch out, Cozy, you're going to bite your tongue if you don't pull it back in!" I yelled. I sat there, laughing to myself. What a sight that Cozy is!

Cozy came to the fence and sat down beside Tony. Jessica threw a few more nuts into the enclosure. The shells were still on the macadamia nuts, and she began hitting them with a rock. Tony and Sampa tried it out, too. Sampa got her nut cracked and ate the delicious meat inside. Tony's mouth was watering, and he was working hard to crack the nut he had claimed. Sampa began helping him and succeeded in cracking it with one of the rocks she had. Tony helped himself to the nut, enjoying every morsel. Cozy was watching all along. Excitedly, he cracked the nut he was given and gobbled it down quickly. He spotted a few more on the ground and worked on those, too. He ate happily.

Later on that afternoon Sally was peeking in an old log on the ground. I went over to the log that she was leaning over.

"Sally, let me show you a trick."

I took a stick and dug into the old log. Very slowly and carefully I pulled it out. Along the bottom of the stick were these lovely and very delicious tasting termites. I gave it to Sally and she ate the insects hardily. "More, Granddad!" she said.

"Here, Sally, it's your turn. You try it."

I heard Phillip talking about changes happening here at our home, a new enclosure that would give us more room to climb and run and play. More like our natural home. Home. Oh, that word; *home.* It is such a wonderful word! Can home get any better than what we have now? Charles, one of our keepers, says it is going to be very soon. I don't know if I am up to the change, but change I will for the good of the group. I have seen a lot of trucks going by lately, Many more than usual around here. Many more humans, too. Zac and I noticed this, but none of the other family members seemed to realize things are changing.

I heard the sound of a familiar truck pull up close by. Eugene was home! Why hadn't he come to see to me? I waited patiently. The keepers called us in to the night rooms. We had our dinner and all fell asleep.

At breakfast time the next morning, everyone ate and headed out to the trees. Everyone but me, that is. I was waiting for Eugene. I didn't understand. Why

hadn't he stopped by to say hello? I'm always so excited to see him. I had to have patience.

Afternoon came, and by that time I had joined the group out by the trees. Eugene came to the fence where Phillip, Jessica, and Charles were all standing. He was looking straight at me. I left my tree log and came to spend some time with him.

As we were sitting at the fence line, he breathed a deep breath. I could tell that he was happy he was finally home again. I felt at peace. I am as happy as I can ever remember being and I will never forget my rescuers. The love they feel for us and the love we feel for them cannot be denied.

They say time is a healer. As I sit here now in my beautiful home, I believe it is true. Time is not the only healer. Humans can be, too. As I have seen for myself, my humans love me and take wonderful care of me now. They love my family that I watch over. When I dream now, I dream of this home. A good, peaceful, loving home. My home, my sanctuary at Chimp Eden.

# Joao

Photo: Courtesy of Jessica Ney

# Acknowledgments

Thank you, Chimp Eden, for all that you do!

Thank you, Jane Goodall Institute-South Africa and Chimp Eden for allowing me to use the real names of the sanctuary, staff, and chimps in this book. The basic stories behind the lives of these chimps are true. I added my own interpretations of situations of the chimps' lives, rescues, and life at the sanctuary.

There are many more sanctuaries in Africa that accommodate these animals and more. They are running out of space and funds rapidly because of the increasing number of chimpanzees that are being confiscated each year in Africa. Natural habitat is being taken away at an alarming rate. Poaching and the bushmeat trade are severe.

I wanted to write this book because of the special place in my heart that I have for animals of all sorts. The true stories of these chimps, from their confinement, rescue, and the rehabilitation at the sanctuary are incredible. In this book, I wanted to give the chimps a voice. To be able to tell the stories of their lives in what I believe they might say if they could speak and understand our language. I want to get the point across that chimps are not human and should never be treated like a human. They are a wild animal and can be very dangerous! They should be treated

44

with respect. The real-life rescues of these chimps are dangerous and stressful. The staff at Chimp Eden each has a valuable and necessary part in the success of the rescues and rehabilitations of the chimps at the sanctuary. They work together as a team. One of the goals the staff has is to help the chimps' live as normal lives as possible. Many have had long years of abuse, starvation, isolation, and more. It takes the dedication of all involved, including the staff that help with the rescues, quarantine areas, and feeding of the chimps. Also included is the staff that has the task of watching chimp behavior for hours and hours. It takes a lot of planning and man–hours, but they get it done for the betterment of the chimps. The Jane Goodall Institute (www.janegoodall.org) works tirelessly to protect chimpanzees and their habitat. They need funds to keep working. Chimp Eden is a part of the Jane Goodall Institute-South Africa and relies on contributions to keep doing what they do so well. The Chimp Eden now has three enclosures and houses approximately thirty-one chimps at this time.

I wanted even our youngest citizens to be aware of the problem that faces the chimpanzee and be able to be a part of the solution. Just by purchasing this book, you have helped! A portion of the royalties from every book sold will go to Chimp Eden.

Helping the chimps can be a fun family project too. You can adopt a chimp, donate, and or become a member of Chimp Eden. Go on to the website at

www.janegoodall.co.za and check out everything they have to offer. You can read the daily observation notes about the chimps, post your questions, and get answers, etc.

You may even want to visit and stay in the beautiful five-star hotel there near the nature reserve and sanctuary. Be a volunteer and actually work at Chimp Eden with one of their volunteer programs. The Jane Goodall Institute also has many other programs including a global environmental and humanitarian program for youth, Jane Goodall's Roots & Shoots (www.rootsandshoots.org) and more.

I would like to introduce you to the staff at Chimpanzee Eden!

Eugene Cussons, Managing Director of Chimp Eden. This book talks about only a few of his many chimp rescues. His lovely wife, Natasha Cussons, is the GR Manager. They have a beautiful daughter Haley, who is Mommy's helper, and probably Daddy's, too.

Phillip Cronje, he is the Sanctuary Manager and has over thirty years of primate experience. Thank you, Phillip, for the extra time you have put in to give me the information I needed to get this book completed! When Joao told Cozy he would see him a lot, he meant it! He is there all the time!

Jessica Ney, Animal Observer/Behaviorist, also writes many of the daily observation notes you can read about on the Web site.

Themba Khosa, Charles Ngwenya, and Siswe Dhlamini are Sanctuary Keepers.

You will see Marc Cronje or Lize Kruger if you visit for a tour.

Nenine De Klerk works in the curio shop. Pauline Stuart, JGI Accountant; Sue Purbrick, Newsletter Editor; Marcus van der Merwe, IT Administrator; and Christopher Langeveldt, IT Programmer.

Chimpanzee Eden/Umhloti is a nature reserve in Nelspruit, Mpumalanga, South Africa.

Last but not least, the Executive Director of the Jane Goodall Institute-South Africa, Margi Brocklehurst. Thank you so much, all of you, for your selfless work.

To Jane Goodall, thank God for *you,* and like my kids would say, YOU ROCK!

Eugene and Phil
Photo: Courtesy of Jessica Ney

Top: Lize, Phillip, Themba, Siswe, and Jessica. Below: Phillip, Marc, Themba, Siswe, and Jessica.
Photos: Courtesy of Jessica Ney

# About the Author

I was a registered nurse for approximately thirteen years and have recently been a volunteer foster parent at the Northwest Florida Wildlife Rehabilitation Institute in Pensacola, Florida, for the past three years.

I am a wife of twenty-four years, married to Major John Ingram, Marine Corps fighter pilot, now retired. We have three children, Melissa, Thomas, and Daniel. They are the loves of my life! I also have a wonderful son-in-law, a Captain in the Air Force, Adam Wasinger, who is currently serving in Iraq.

LaVergne, TN USA
23 April 2010
180302LV00002B